Who Is
J. K. Rowling?

An Unauthorized Biography

Who Is
J. K. Rowling?

by Pam Pollack and Meg Belviso

illustrated by Stephen Marchesi

Penguin Workshop
An Imprint of Penguin Random House

To Meg, my partner, whose creative genius
I will always respect—PP
To all the great friends I've made in Harry Potter fandom
—MB
For Chris and Alex, ten years on—SM

PENGUIN WORKSHOP
Penguin Young Readers Group
An Imprint of Penguin Random House LLC

Text copyright © 2012 by Pamela D. Pollack and Margaret Dean Belviso. Illustrations copyright © 2012 by Stephen Marchesi. Cover illustration copyright © 2012 by Penguin Random House LLC. All rights reserved. Published by Penguin Workshop, an imprint of Penguin Random House LLC, 345 Hudson Street, New York, New York 10014. PENGUIN and PENGUIN WORKSHOP are trademarks of Penguin Books Ltd. WHO HQ & Design is a registered trademark of Penguin Random House LLC. Printed in the USA.

Library of Congress Control Number: 2012001406

ISBN 9780448458724

30 29 28 27 26

WRZL

Contents

Who Is
J. K. Rowling?

Do you know what a Muggle is? Do you know how to get to Platform 9 ¾? Do you have a favorite Bertie Bott's Every Flavor Bean?

Muggles, Platform 9 ¾, and Bertie Bott's Every Flavor Beans were all created by one person: J. K. Rowling.

Jo, as she has been called since she was little, always wanted to be a writer. But being a writer would not be easy. What if

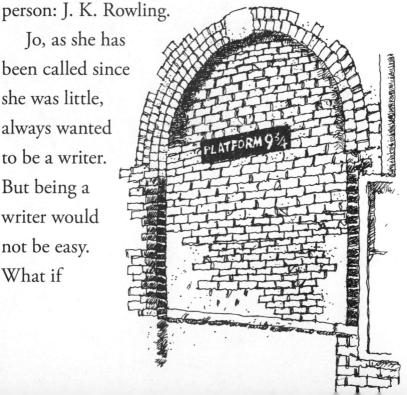

no one wanted to buy her stories? So after she finished school in her early twenties, she got a job as a secretary in London, England. Jo made enough money to pay her bills.

Every day she filed papers and made copies. The next day was always the same as the last.

UNITED KINGDOM

But in her heart, she was still a writer. In her spare moments, she typed stories on her computer. She scribbled the names of imaginary people and places on the backs of papers. The stories didn't earn her any money. Still, she couldn't stop writing them.

Writing stories also let Jo forget about the sad things in her life. Like her mother being very sick.

One weekend Jo took a trip to Manchester, a city in northern England. She was going to move there, and she needed a place to live. She had a long train ride back to London. She stared out the window, thinking of nothing.

Suddenly a picture of a boy popped into her head. He had round glasses and a scar shaped like a lightning bolt.

Jo reached into her bag. She wanted to write down everything about him. But she didn't have a pen. She turned back to the window and thought more about the boy. He was a wizard, but he didn't know it. He lived with a family who was not his real family. They kept his magic a secret. They hoped to squash it out of him. But the boy's magic was too strong.

As the train sped through the English countryside, more people crowded into Jo's head. They were people the boy knew. There was a ghost named Nearly Headless Nick. And a best friend with red hair. And a clever girl named Hermione.

By the time Jo reached London, she had a whole new world in her head. One day, she hoped, she could write a book about it. When she got

home she found a pen. She pulled out a notebook.
On the first page she wrote the name of the boy
with the lightning bolt scar.

His name was Harry Potter.

Chapter 1
Make-Believe

Joanne Rowling always loved trains. Maybe it was because her parents met on a train. It was a chilly day, and her mother, Anne, said she was cold. A stranger named Peter offered her his coat. A year later they were married.

Jo was born at Yate
General Hospital on July 31,
1965, in Gloucestershire,
England. Two years later
she had a little sister named
Diana, or Di.

Jo made up stories to tell her little sister.
In one story, Di fell down a rabbit hole. Luckily
the family of rabbits who lived in the hole fed her
strawberries. As they got older, Jo and Di played

games. Their favorite was the cliff game. In that game, Jo dangled from the top stair of the staircase. She pretended she was on a cliff. She pleaded with Di to rescue her before she fell. But Di never helped. Finally Jo would fall to the floor, "dead." Then they would start all over again. Only this time Di would be the one hanging off the cliff.

When they weren't playing games, Jo and Di were often fighting. During one fight, Jo threw a battery at her sister, leaving a scar just above her eyebrow.

"I didn't mean to hit her," Jo explained to her mother. "I thought she would duck." But this excuse didn't stop her mother from being angrier than Jo had ever seen her.

When Jo was nine, her family moved to a little village called Tutshill. Tutshill sits on the eastern bank of the River

Wye. It is also near a big forest called the Forest of Dean. Perhaps even better than the river and the forest was an old castle on a cliff not far from Jo's house! It is called the Chepstow Castle.

CHEPSTOW CASTLE

IN 1066, WILLIAM OF NORMANDY CROSSED THE CHANNEL FROM FRANCE TO INVADE ENGLAND. ONCE HE BECAME KING, WILLIAM STARTED BUILDING CASTLES ALL OVER ENGLAND. CHEPSTOW WAS THE VERY FIRST CASTLE HE BUILT. IT WAS IN AN IMPORTANT SPOT. THE CASTLE GUARDED THE MAIN RIVER CROSSING FROM ENGLAND INTO WALES. HUNDREDS OF YEARS EARLIER, THE ROMANS HAD A FORT IN THE SAME PLACE. WILLIAM USED BRICKS FROM THE ROMAN FORT IN THE MAIN ARCHWAY OF HIS CASTLE. IT IS THE OLDEST MEDIEVAL CASTLE IN GREAT BRITAIN. IT CONTAINS WHAT IS PROBABLY THE OLDEST MEDIEVAL TOILET!

Living in the country was a dream come true for Jo's parents, who were both from London. Her mother was a lab technician. Her father worked at an aircraft engine plant.

The river, the forest, and the castle gave Jo even more ideas for her stories. So did the many books she read. Some of her favorites were *The Little White Horse*, a story about a girl who ends a long feud in her magical family, and *The Chronicles of Narnia*, about a group of children who rule a secret, magical kingdom.

One thing that Jo didn't like about Tutshill was her school, Tutshill Primary. Her teacher, Mrs. Morgan, was very strict. As Jo remembered, she seated all the children in her class according to how smart she thought they were. The bright students sat on Mrs. Morgan's left. The students Mrs. Morgan thought were "dim" sat on her right. On the first day of class, Mrs. Morgan gave everyone a test on fractions. Jo had never studied fractions before. She failed the test. Mrs. Morgan made Jo sit on the "bad" side of the room. In an

article called "The Not Especially Fascinating Life
So Far of J. K. Rowling," Jo said she sat "as far right
as you could get without sitting in the playground."

Jo always remembered how awful she felt that
day. She didn't think the test was fair. Years later,
she would write about another teacher, Severus
Snape, doing similar things to Harry Potter.

Jo wasn't sad to leave Tutshill Primary behind.
At 11, she went to Wyedean Comprehensive
School. At first Jo was afraid. She'd heard some
scary stories about what happened to students
there. For instance, she heard that they stuffed
new students' heads down the toilets the first day.

No one stuck Jo's head down the toilet at

Wyedean. But one of the toughest girls in school did pick a fight with her. Even though Jo was quiet and a good student, she fought back against the bigger girl. She became famous for standing up to

the bully. But standing up to the bully came with a price. In "Not Especially," Jo said that she spent the next few weeks "peering nervously around corners" in case the bully was waiting for her.

Jo didn't like fighting in real life. But she loved fighting battles in her imagination. At lunchtime she told her friends stories in which they were the heroes. Made-up adventures, Jo was discovering, could be more fun than the real thing.

Chapter 2
A Flying Car

In many ways, Jo was a lot like Harry's brainy friend, Hermione Granger. Jo once told a group of students at a school in Montclair, New Jersey, that she herself was "never as clever or as annoying" as Hermione. Yet she could be a know-it-all on the outside while inside she was very insecure. She also got good grades in school like Hermione did.

Then she discovered a new favorite writer: Jane Austen.

JANE AUSTEN

JANE AUSTEN WAS WRITING BOOKS ALMOST TWO HUNDRED YEARS BEFORE J. K. ROWLING STARTED WRITING ABOUT HARRY POTTER. JANE AUSTEN WROTE SIX NOVELS: *SENSE & SENSIBILITY*, *PRIDE & PREJUDICE*, *MANSFIELD PARK*, *EMMA*, *PERSUASION*, AND *NORTHANGER ABBEY*. ALL SIX HAVE BECOME CLASSICS AND HAVE BEEN MADE INTO MOVIES—SOME MORE THAN ONCE.

JANE AUSTEN WAS JO'S FAVORITE AUTHOR. JO'S FAVORITE BOOK WAS *EMMA*, WHICH SHE CALLED "THE MOST SKILLFULLY MANAGED MYSTERY I'VE EVER READ." IT WAS THE SAME KIND OF MYSTERY THAT JO WOULD LATER WRITE HERSELF, A STORY WHERE THE MAIN CHARACTER COMES TO REALIZE THAT SHE HAS THE WRONG IDEA ABOUT EVERYTHING. THE MAIN CHARACTER— AND THE READER—MUST GO BACK TO THE BEGINNING IN ORDER TO SEE THINGS THE WAY THEY REALLY ARE. HARRY DOES THE SAME THING IN *HARRY POTTER AND THE SORCERER'S STONE*. HE COMES TO UNDERSTAND THAT PROFESSOR SNAPE WAS NOT HURTING HIM BUT ACTUALLY PROTECTING HIM.

ONE OF JO'S CHARACTERS—FILCH'S CAT, MRS. NORRIS—IS NAMED AFTER A BUSYBODY IN JANE AUSTEN'S *MANSFIELD PARK*.

Jo loved the way Austen put clues in her books about what was going to happen that the reader didn't notice until the end. It made her want to read the books over and over again. She tried to learn how to do the same thing in her own stories.

At fifteen, Jo was still imagining exciting adventures in faraway places. Her own life in Tutshill went on the same as always. Then everything changed. Her mother was sick. Anne had multiple sclerosis, or MS, a disease that damages nerves. There is no cure for MS. Jo's mother got weaker every day. It was hard seeing

her so sick. Jo was especially close to her mother. Her father was often at work so Jo depended on her mother.

Some people didn't want to be around her mother because of her illness. Years later, Jo would create a character with an incurable illness in her books. She wanted to show how thoughtless people could be around someone who was very sick.

Even when Jo was feeling very sad about her mother, she had one friend who could always make her laugh. His name was Seán Harris, and he was the real-life inspiration for Ron Weasley. Besides being loyal and fun, Seán was the first one of Jo's friends to get a driver's license. He had a car—a turquoise Ford Anglia. When Jo was feeling down,

they would zoom off into the countryside. Jo told Seán about her dreams of being a writer, a secret she had never shared with anyone else. He believed she would be a success.

Years later, when Jo wrote her second book, *Harry Potter and the Chamber of Secrets*, she gave Seán's car a starring role. The car rescues Harry just as it had rescued Jo—only in Jo's imagination the car could fly.

If Seán was the inspiration for Ron Weasley, Jo's teacher John Nettleship was the person who inspired the character of Severus Snape. Mr. Nettleship was strict like Jo's old teacher Mrs. Morgan. He was also lanky with long, black hair and a sharp tongue, just like Harry's professor. His chemistry class was full of "bangs and smells," and it was far from Jo's favorite. On a report card, he described Jo as "a daydreamer who never answered questions about science and hated taking part in experiments." Jo much preferred her classes in English and foreign languages to chemistry.

In her last year at Wyedean, Jo was chosen by her teachers to be Head Girl. This was the highest honor a student could have. The Head Boy and Girl represented the school at events, sometimes making speeches.

When teachers were called out of the classroom, the Head Boy and Girl were in charge of keeping other students under control.

After leaving Wyedean in 1983, Jo attended the University of Exeter. Her favorite subject had always been English literature. But she thought knowing French might lead to a better

UNIVERSITY OF EXETER

job after college. So Jo studied French, Latin, and Greek. She even spent a year in Paris as a teaching assistant. But secretly Jo only wanted to write. Her favorite thing about studying languages was learning new words and thinking up names for the characters in her stories, like Voldemort and Malfoy. In French, *mort* means death, *mal* means bad, and *foy* comes from *foi* which means faith.

CHARACTER NAMES

YOU CAN TELL A LOT ABOUT THE HARRY POTTER CHARACTERS FROM THEIR NAMES.

THE WEASLEY FAMILY—HARRY'S FAVORITE FAMILY IS NAMED AFTER ONE OF JO'S FAVORITE ANIMALS, THE WEASEL.

REMUS LUPIN—REMUS SHARES HIS FIRST NAME WITH ONE OF TWO MYTHICAL BROTHERS (ROMULUS AND REMUS) WHO WERE RAISED BY A WOLF AND FOUNDED ROME. HIS LAST NAME COMES FROM *LUPINE*, WHICH MEANS WOLFLIKE.

FENRIR GREYBACK—THE SERIES' SECOND WEREWOLF GETS HIS NAME FROM FENRISÚLFR (FENRIS WOLF), A NORSE WOLF GOD.

SIRIUS BLACK—SIRIUS IS NAMED AFTER THE DOG STAR. VERY FITTING FOR A MAN WHO CAN TURN INTO A DOG!

ALBUS DUMBLEDORE—ALBUS COMES FROM THE LATIN WORD FOR WHITE. DUMBLEDORE IS AN OLD ENGLISH WORD MEANING BUMBLEBEE. JO NAMED HIM THAT BECAUSE SHE IMAGINED THE OLD HEADMASTER HUMMING TO HIMSELF LIKE A BEE.

RITA SKEETER—HARRY IS OFTEN ANNOYED BY REPORTER RITA SKEETER. NOT SURPRISING, SINCE *SKEETER* IS A SLANG WORD FOR MOSQUITO.

PEEVES—PEEVES THE POLTERGEIST LOVES PLAYING PRANKS AT HOGWARTS. HE'S LIVING UP TO HIS NAME, WHICH MEANS TO IRRITATE.

Chapter 3
On the Move

When Jo graduated in 1987 she moved to Clapham, a neighborhood in South London. For a while she worked as a secretary at Amnesty International, which fights for the fair treatment of people in different countries all over the world. Jo felt like she was helping people in trouble.

AMNESTY INTERNATIONAL

LIKE HARRY POTTER, JO ALWAYS BELIEVED PEOPLE SHOULD BE TREATED FAIRLY—EVER SINCE THE DAYS WHEN SHE STOOD UP TO THE SCHOOL BULLY OR GOT ANGRY AT HER TEACHERS. AMNESTY IS AN INTERNATIONAL ORGANIZATION THAT FIGHTS FOR THE RIGHTS OF OTHERS, ESPECIALLY FOR PEOPLE WHO HAVE BEEN PUT IN JAIL FOR THEIR BELIEFS. IN 1979, FOR INSTANCE, PEOPLE IN ARGENTINA WHO CRITICIZED THE NEW GOVERNMENT STARTED TO DISAPPEAR. AMNESTY WORKED TO TELL EVERYONE WHAT WAS GOING ON AND STOP IT. THE GROUP ALSO STEPS IN ANYWHERE CHILDREN ARE MISTREATED OR DENIED AN EDUCATION.

Still, Jo's favorite part of the workday was her lunch hour. She could concentrate completely on her stories then. It was just like her days at Wyedean. Only now, instead of telling stories to

her friends, she wrote down the stories. She tried writing several novels for adults but never finished them.

Back home in Tutshill, her mother wasn't getting any better. Jo worried about her a lot. She decided she needed a change. She wanted to leave London for someplace new. She chose Manchester, a city in northern England. It was a bit farther away from her family, but she could still visit them often. On the weekends she took the train from

London to Manchester to look at flats, which are what people in England call apartments. It was on one of these weekend train trips in 1990 that she got the idea for her greatest story yet: Harry Potter.

Once Harry "fell into her head," Jo could think about little else. Her new flat in Manchester was full of notes about Harry and his world. One evening Jo had a big fight with her boyfriend. She went to a nearby pub, a place where people

gathered to eat and drink. Alone at a table, she thought about how satisfying it would be to smack something at her boyfriend's head. Maybe a big iron ball. Perhaps while flying on a broomstick! Jo had just created a new game that only wizards could play. She called it Quidditch.

Not long after Jo got the idea for Harry Potter, her mother died. Even though Anne had been sick for a long time, neither Jo nor her sister or father had ever really believed she would die. It was too terrible to imagine. Now it had happened.

Jo hoped living in another country would lift her spirits. So she took a job teaching English in Oporto, Portugal. She also hoped that her new job

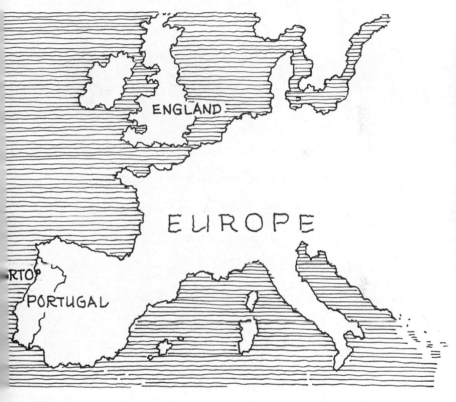

would leave her more time for her book. During her first weeks in Portugal, Jo wrote a new chapter that became one of her favorites in the whole series.

In this chapter, Harry discovers the Mirror of Erised. The mirror shows anyone who looks in it their greatest desire. When Harry looks in the mirror, he sees the mother and father that he never knew. If Jo could have looked in the Mirror of Erised, she thought she would probably see her mother.

While in Portugal, she met a journalist named Jorge Arantes. They fell in love and were married a few months later in 1992. The next year Jo had a baby girl named Jessica. Jo loved her new baby, but her marriage didn't make her happy.

She left Jorge and Portugal in 1993, taking baby Jessica, boxes of Harry Potter notes, and three completed chapters of *Harry Potter and the Philosopher's Stone*.

Chapter 4
First Draft

Jo and baby Jessica went to live in Edinburgh, Scotland. Jo's sister, Di, was already living there with her husband. More than anything, Jo wanted to finish her book. Every time Jessica fell asleep, Jo pulled out her notes and wrote—usually in coffee shops and cafés. She wrote as much and as fast as she could.

Because she didn't have a job yet, Jo lived on public assistance. This meant that the government sent a check each month for rent and food. Sometimes there was only enough money to buy food for Jessica, and Jo went hungry. While Jo was struggling to make ends meet, the government in England started a campaign called Back to Basics. It said that single mothers like Jo were something the country should be ashamed of. Jo vowed that if she ever had money to spare, she would use it to help women like her who had to take care of children on their own.

Luckily, Jo had friends to help her. When she needed a place to write, she went to Nicolson's Restaurant, where the owner, Di's husband, let her sit for hours with Jessica. Jo's old friend Seán lent her money to get a flat. With her friends' and family's encouragement, Jo finally finished *Harry*

Potter and the Philosopher's Stone. It was only a first draft. She knew she would have to make a lot of changes before it was good enough to be published.

She shared it with Di, who had always been the first to hear her stories. Di loved it. Jo got a job as a French teacher. When she wasn't teaching, she spent time working on her manuscript. She worked very hard. She wanted to make it as good

as it could be. Jo wrote and rewrote every chapter.
Finally, seven years after Jo first had the idea of
Harry Potter, she was ready to show her book to
the world.

Chapter 5
The Slush Pile

Jo printed out the first three chapters and put them in a plastic cover. She sent them to an agent. If the agent liked the first three chapters, then Jo would send the rest of the book. An agent is a person who sells books to publishers for authors. Agents have the contacts at publishing companies that beginning writers don't. The agent gets a part of whatever money the author makes. Jo knew that she had a much better chance of selling her book if she had an agent. Only a couple of days after she sent it, Jo received her manuscript back in the mail. The agent did not want to read the rest of it.

CHRISTOPHER LITTLE

Could all her hard work have been for nothing? What if nobody ever wanted to read the story? But she had come so far, she couldn't imagine giving up. She looked for another agent. She found a man named Christopher Little. Jo had always loved names, and she especially liked his name because Little sounded like the name of a character in a children's book. Jo put her three chapters into an envelope again and waited.

The manuscript landed in the slush pile at the agency where Christopher Little worked.

47

A slush pile is the name for the many books and stories that just arrive in the offices of agents and publishers. Nobody has asked to see them; the stories in the slush pile are almost always by beginners who haven't yet had a book published.

Slush piles can be very large. Usually Christopher Little wouldn't spend too much time going through the slush pile. But one day as he was heading out to meet someone for lunch, he picked up a story from the slush pile that other people in the office had liked. He took it with him to the restaurant. When his friend was late, he pulled it out and started reading about a boy wizard.

Little was quickly sucked into the world of Hogwarts. When he got back to the office, he sent Jo a letter. In it, he thanked her for sending the story and said he was eager to sell it. When Jo received the letter, she couldn't believe it. It was only two sentences long, but it was the greatest letter she'd ever received.

Christopher Little sold Jo's book to Bloomsbury
Publishers. She couldn't wait to tell her family,
especially Di, who had always loved Jo's stories
more than anyone. With the money from the sale,

Jo stopped teaching French and got right back to work on Harry Potter. She had big plans for her boy wizard.

Chapter 6
Pottermania

After years of dreaming and years of hard work, Jo was going to be a published author. She still almost couldn't believe it. Then one evening, about a month later, she got more exciting news: Christopher Little told her that in the United States the book was being sold in an auction.

Jo was confused. Wasn't an auction just for paintings or jewelry or expensive pieces of furniture? At auctions, people called out prices that they were willing to pay for things. These offers were called bids. How could anyone be bidding on her story?

Mr. Little explained that there were publishers in America that were interested in Harry Potter— *very* interested. So interested that they were competing with one another to buy it, each publisher trying to top the others' bids. Just like in the auctions Jo knew. "The price is up to five figures," he said. That meant over $10,000. Two hours later Mr. Little called back. The price was now up to six figures. That meant Jo's book would be sold for over $100,000.

The winner was Arthur A. Levine of Scholastic. He was a little scared about spending so much money on a first-time author. But he loved the book so much. He thought kids in America would, too. His favorite thing about Harry Potter was "the idea of growing up unappreciated, feeling outcast, and then this great satisfaction of being discovered."

ARTHUR A. LEVINE

Jo understood the feeling of being discovered. With her newfound wealth she bought a new jacket. It was strange for Jo to be able to spend money on herself and not worry about it.

In June 1997, *Harry Potter and the Philosopher's Stone* by J. K. Rowling was published in the United Kingdom. Bloomsbury had asked Jo if they could use her initials instead of her name on the book. They were worried that boys might not want to read the book if it was written by a woman! Jo didn't have a middle name, so she gave herself one: Kathleen, after her grandmother. That's where the *K* in J. K. comes from.

Bloomsbury didn't keep the secret of her being a woman for long. *Harry Potter and the Philosopher's Stone* was a big hit. Jo's own daughter, Jessica, was only four—too young to read the book—but other children loved it. Jo was voted the winner of the Smarties Book Prize by schoolchildren all over the United Kingdom.

They couldn't wait to read her second book, which Jo had already finished: *Harry Potter and the Chamber of Secrets.* It was published in July 1998.

Jo was also becoming famous in America, where her book was called *Harry Potter and the Sorcerer's Stone.* Scholastic changed the title so everyone would know that the book had magic in it.

Americans and British people both speak English. But there are a lot of differences in the ways they speak it. For American kids, some changes were made in the Harry Potter books including Scotch Tape for Sellotape, parking lot for car park, and bag of chips for packet of crisps. This kind of "Americanizing" is done in many US editions of books that were first published in the United Kingdom.

In October 1998, Jo traveled to the United States for the first time for a ten-day book tour. At first Jo was worried that American children wouldn't like her book as much as children in the United Kingdom did. But she was wrong. "When I did public readings," she told *The Scotsman* newspaper, "they even all laughed in the same places as British youngsters."

Jo was surprised that many of the children she met had already read *Harry Potter and the Chamber of Secrets*. The book wasn't even

published in the United States yet. They had ordered the book from England on the Internet because they couldn't wait.

Jo was more successful than she had ever dreamed—but things were just getting started. In the publishing world, no children's books had ever been as popular as the Harry Potter books. Each book landed on the *New York Times* Best Seller list and stayed there for so long that the newspaper started running a separate list for children's literature. Even popular children's book writers like Dr. Seuss (*The Cat in the Hat*), R. L. Stine (*Goosebumps*), and C. S. Lewis (*The Chronicles of Narnia*) did not sell as many books.

By the time she returned to the United States to promote her third book, *Harry Potter and the Prisoner of Azkaban*, Jo was met by, not just children, but crowds of adults. Why were so many adults reading a book written for children? It's because a really good story appeals to people of all ages. The press called it Pottermania. It meant that everyone was going crazy for Harry Potter. Jo's life had changed beyond her wildest dreams.

She traveled around the world and stayed in the best hotels. She could buy clothes made by famous fashion designers. Once, while going to a movie premiere, she wore a pair of gold shoes. They had six-inch heels and cost one thousand dollars.

What was happening to Jo was a little bit like what happens to Harry when he first arrives at Hogwarts. He is surprised to learn he is famous. People he doesn't know want to be his friend. Harry often finds his name in the newspapers. Now Jo was in the papers, too—and on the radio and on TV. Reporters even showed up at her house. Perhaps some of the reporters she met influenced the way Jo wrote Rita Skeeter,

a devious reporter who makes up stories about Harry.

Jo did not know that being an author would be like this. In an article in the *Independent* newspaper, she said, "I imagined being a famous writer would be like being Jane Austen, being able to sit at home in the parsonage and your books would be very famous. I never dreamed it would impact my daughter's life negatively, which at times it has."

Jessica was now seven years old, and she still
had never read any of her mother's books. Jo
thought the Harry Potter books were for readers
who were at least eight years old. But Jessica could
not stand being the only person at school who had
never read them. So Jo read them to her—and she
loved them.

Jessica did not love having strangers snap her picture without asking if they could. Neither did her mother. On a vacation in the Galapagos Islands, a photographer took pictures of Jo in a bikini. Jo didn't like that, either.

Everyone wanted to know all about the Rowling family: Jo, Jessica, and Jo's new boyfriend,

Dr. Neil Murray. A friend introduced Jo to Neil in 2000. With his dark hair and glasses, Neil looked like a grown-up Harry Potter. When he and Jo started dating, the press began snapping pictures of him, too. Jo and Neil were planning a life together with Jessica. In 2001, they bought a nineteenth-century mansion on the banks of the

River Tay in Scotland. Besides having a morning room, a drawing room, and 162 acres of land, the

house was close to Castle Menzies. Castle Menzies
is about five hundred years old. Many people

think it looks a lot like Hogwarts.

Jo loved her new life, but sometimes being famous was hard. Jo was by nature very private, and it was scary to feel like she was being spied on. She had never planned on being famous. In an interview, she said, "I never wanted it and I never expected it and certainly never worked for it, and I see it as something I have to get through really."

Pottermania was getting bigger and bigger. It was only a matter of time before Hollywood got in on the game.

Chapter 7
Challenges!

Harry Potter was a worldwide phenomenon by 2001. Four books in the series had already been published. When a new book came out, bookstores held parties. Fans lined up for hours,

sometimes wearing costumes, so they could buy the book the minute it went on sale at midnight.

But Hollywood movie studios were not at all sure the books would work as films. Sure, people loved Harry Potter, but would they go to see a movie with no parts for American movie stars? Some people in Hollywood even suggested making Harry American. Jo would not allow it. Harry was British and so was his world. Also, there was so much magic in the books. Re-creating the magic through special effects would be very expensive. Film companies did not want to spend a lot of money on a movie without being sure people would pay to see it.

And not everyone was a fan of the books. In the United States, Harry Potter was one of the most challenged books of the decade. A book is "challenged" when a parent or a group of people demand that it be kept out of schools and public libraries.

CHALLENGED BOOKS

MANY OF THE MOST WELL-KNOWN AND BELOVED BOOKS HAVE BEEN CHALLENGED AS BEING BAD FOR CHILDREN. BESIDES THE HARRY POTTER SERIES, OTHER COMMONLY CHALLENGED BOOKS INCLUDE:

ADVENTURES OF HUCKLEBERRY FINN BY MARK TWAIN— THIS BOOK HAS BEEN CHALLENGED FOR ITS RACIALLY CHARGED LANGUAGE.

1984 BY GEORGE ORWELL—ORWELL'S NOVEL WAS BANNED IN THE SOVIET UNION FOR BEING ANTICOMMUNIST. IT WAS BANNED IN THE UNITED STATES FOR BEING PRO-COMMUNIST.

BRIDGE TO TERABITHIA BY KATHERINE PATERSON—SOME VIEWED THE IMAGINARY WORLD BUILT BY TWO CHILDREN AS DANGEROUS AND UNCHRISTIAN.

THE GIVER BY LOIS LOWRY—THIS NEWBERY MEDAL WINNER IS MOST FREQUENTLY CHALLENGED BECAUSE IN ITS FICTIONAL WORLD, PEOPLE ARE KILLED FOR NOT BEING PERFECT.

IN THE NIGHT KITCHEN BY MAURICE SENDAK— THE TODDLER HERO IN THIS BOOK DOESN'T WEAR CLOTHES FOR MUCH OF THE STORY.

LORD OF THE FLIES BY WILLIAM GOLDING— MANY PEOPLE OBJECT TO HOW VIOLENT THE CHILDREN IN THIS BOOK BECOME.

THE STUPIDS BY HARRY ALLARD—THIS BOOK IS ABOUT A VERY DIM-WITTED FAMILY. SOME FEEL IT ENCOURAGES KIDS TO DISOBEY THEIR PARENTS.

CAPTAIN UNDERPANTS BY DAV PILKEY—THIS BOOK HAS TOO MUCH "BATHROOM TALK" AND BAD BEHAVIOR FOR SOME PARENTS.

Why did these people think the Harry Potter books were bad for children? It was because the hero was a wizard. They believed that Jo's books were promoting witchcraft in real life. Of course, the magic in Harry Potter isn't real. All the spells and potions in the books were made up by Jo. The names were ones she created, too. Spells like *Accio* (which brings an object to a wizard), *Expecto Patronum* (which calls forth a wizard's guardian spirit), and *Confundo* (which confuses a person) are all based on Latin words. However, many of the ingredients that Harry uses in his potions class such as dittany, belladonna, and hellebore are real.

HELLEBORE

In Michigan, a school superintendent forbade teachers from reading Harry Potter aloud to their classes. School librarians were told to take it off the shelves. In Pennsylvania, a mother tried to get the books banned from all the schools in her district. A church in New Mexico burned copies of Harry Potter because they didn't want anyone to read them. The books were also challenged in other countries, like the United Kingdom and Australia.

Many schools in America had "opt-out" policies. That meant that if parents didn't approve of a book that was being taught, their children could leave the class. So in some schools, Harry Potter was only read to classes where every parent said it was okay. Other teachers and librarians stopped recommending Harry Potter to avoid trouble. But no challenge ever kept kids away from Harry Potter. Especially after Warner Brothers Studios finally took a chance on the books.

HERBS

JO LEARNED ABOUT MANY OF THE HERBS AND PLANTS MENTIONED IN HARRY POTTER IN *CULPEPER'S COMPLETE HERBAL*. IT WAS WRITTEN IN THE SEVENTEENTH CENTURY AND IS STILL IN PRINT TODAY.

BELLADONNA

BELLADONNA—IN THE MIDDLE AGES, THIS POISONOUS PLANT WAS THOUGHT TO BE A KEY INGREDIENT IN WITCH'S FLYING OINTMENT. AT HOGWARTS, IT IS A PART OF THE STANDARD POTION-MAKING KIT THAT ALL STUDENTS HAVE.

DEATH CAP—THIS POISONOUS MUSHROOM IS BELIEVED TO CAUSE MOST MUSHROOM DEATHS WORLDWIDE. IT IS THE MAIN INGREDIENT IN THE DEATH CAP DRAUGHT.

DITTANY—THIS FLOWERING PLANT WAS OFTEN USED FOR HEALING. SOME VARIETIES CAN BE USED TO FLAVOR FOOD. THE STUDENTS AT HOGWARTS USE IT TO HEAL CUTS.

DITTANY

LOVAGE—THIS PLANT
IS A LOT LIKE CELERY.
THE LEAVES ARE USED
IN COOKING AND TO
HELP DIGESTION. AT
HOGWARTS, IT IS USED
IN THE BREWING
OF BEFUDDLEMENT
DRAUGHTS.

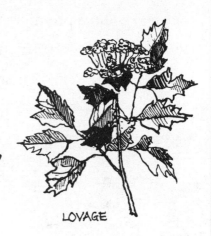

LOVAGE

NETTLE

NETTLE—THIS
WIDESPREAD PLANT
IS KNOWN FOR ITS
STINGING HAIRS
AND IS SOMETIMES
BREWED IN TEA.
FRESH NETTLES
ARE USED IN THE
BOIL-CURE POTION.

The movie version of *Harry Potter and the Sorcerer's Stone* premiered in November 2001. It was a hit! American audiences had no trouble accepting the very British story starring British

actors. Every one of the Harry Potter books would be made into a film. One book, *Harry Potter and the Deathly Hallows*, would even be split into two films.

Jo was excited about the movie. But she was more excited about her upcoming marriage to Neil Murray. They planned to wed in the Galapagos Islands at the end of 2001. But they canceled that wedding when their plans were leaked to the press. Jo didn't want any reporters spying on her on her wedding day.

So Jo and Neil got married in the library of their home in Perthshire, Scotland. There were only fifteen guests, including Jo's father and his second wife. Jo had three bridesmaids: Jessica, Di, and Neil's sister, Lorna. Jo couldn't wait to begin this new chapter in her life.

STARS OF THE FILMS

DANIEL RADCLIFFE AS HARRY POTTER

DANIEL RADCLIFFE WAS JUST ELEVEN YEARS OLD WHEN HE WAS CAST AS HARRY POTTER. HE SOON BECAME ALMOST AS FAMOUS AS THE CHARACTER HE PLAYED. HE STARRED IN ALL EIGHT HARRY POTTER MOVIES. HE HAD ALWAYS WANTED TO BE AN ACTOR, AND HE TRIED TO LEARN AS MUCH AS HE COULD FROM THE OLDER STARS THAT PLAYED HIS TEACHERS AT HOGWARTS. WHEN HE WAS SEVENTEEN, HE STARRED IN A PLAY CALLED *EQUUS*. RICHARD GRIFFITHS, WHO PLAYED HARRY'S MUGGLE UNCLE, VERNON, IN THE MOVIES, WAS ALSO IN IT. IN 2011 DANIEL CAME BACK TO BROADWAY TO STAR IN *HOW TO SUCCEED IN BUSINESS WITHOUT REALLY TRYING*. NOW HE HAD TO SING AND LEARN TO SPEAK WITH AN AMERICAN ACCENT.

EMMA WATSON AS HERMIONE GRANGER

EMMA WATSON WAS BORN IN PARIS, FRANCE. WHEN SHE WAS FIVE YEARS OLD, HER FAMILY MOVED TO ENGLAND. SHE WAS NINE YEARS OLD WHEN SHE TRIED OUT FOR THE ROLE OF HERMIONE. SHE WON IT OVER THOUSANDS OF OTHER GIRLS. UNLIKE HERMIONE, EMMA IS VERY INTERESTED IN FASHION. SHE HAS APPEARED ON THE COVER OF FASHION MAGAZINES LIKE *VOGUE* AND *ELLE*. AFTER RECEIVING GOOD GRADES AT SCHOOL IN ENGLAND, EMMA MOVED TO AMERICA TO GO TO BROWN UNIVERSITY. HERMIONE WOULD BE PROUD.

RUPERT GRINT AS RON WEASLEY

RON WEASLEY IS THE SECOND YOUNGEST OF
SEVEN, BUT RUPERT GRINT IS THE OLDEST OF FIVE.
GROWING UP, HE WENT TO DRAMA CLASSES AND
PLAYED RUMPLESTILTSKIN IN A LOCAL PLAY. BUT
NOTHING COMPARED TO STARTING WORK ON THE
HARRY POTTER MOVIES WHEN HE WAS TWELVE.
RUPERT MADE A NUMBER OF OTHER MOVIES WHILE
WORKING ON THE SERIES INCLUDING *CHERRYBOMB*,
WHERE HE PLAYED A TOUGH CHARACTER NOT AT
ALL LIKE RON.

Chapter 8
Truly Magical

Jo's family was growing fast. In 2003, she gave birth to David Gordon Rowling Murray. Two years later, she had another daughter. Her name was Mackenzie Jean Rowling Murray. While she was pregnant with Mackenzie, Jo was hard at

work on the sixth Harry Potter book, *Harry Potter and the Half-Blood Prince.* It was published when Mackenzie was seven months old. Jo dedicated the book to her "beautiful daughter."

The Rowling-Murrays lived mostly in Scotland. Along with the house on the banks of

the River Tay, they owned a seventeenth-century mansion in Edinburgh. The Edinburgh house had thirty-one rooms. It was guarded by high fences, electric gates, and closed-circuit televisions. Jo also hired a bodyguard who had served in the British Special Air Service to protect her family.

When the family went to London they stayed
in their third house, which had an underground
pool and twenty-four-hour security.

The Harry Potter books had made Jo very rich. She was the second highest-earning female entertainer in the world (after Oprah Winfrey). *Forbes Magazine* estimated her worth at over a billion dollars. *The Sunday Times* in England listed her as the 122nd richest person in Britain—that put her eleven places ahead of the Queen of England!

On January 11, 2007, in the Balmoral Hotel in Edinburgh, J. K. Rowling finished the last book in the Harry Potter series. In her hotel room, there was a bust of the Greek god Hermes. At the bottom of the bust, Jo wrote, "J. K. Rowling finished writing *Harry Potter and the Deathly Hallows* in this room (652) on 11th January 2007."

The final book was published on July 21 that same year. So much had happened in Jo's life since she first started thinking about the boy wizard. She had gone from a poor, single mother who didn't have enough money to buy food to being richer than the Queen of England. She had a new husband and three children. She was famous all over the world—just like Harry Potter himself. The real King's Cross train station in London now had a sign leading to platform 9 ¾ with a luggage cart

wheeled halfway through the magical barrier. At Nicolson's Restaurant, there was a plaque on the wall that read, "J. K. Rowling wrote some of the early chapters of Harry Potter in the rooms on the first floor of this building."

Despite all the changes in her life, Jo hadn't forgotten the issues that were important to her. She used her money to help the people she had always wanted to help. She volunteered and donated money to charities like Gingerbread, which helps out one-parent families, the National MS Society, which raises money to find a cure for multiple sclerosis, and Amnesty International. She even wrote books for charity. *Fantastic Beasts and Where to Find Them* was Harry's Hogwarts textbook about magical animals—complete with handwritten notes from Harry, Ron, and Hermione. She also wrote *Quidditch Through the Ages*, a history of the magical sport Harry played. The money from the sales of these books went to Comic Relief, which fights poverty all over the world.

For an auction for Book Aid International, which sends books to children in Africa, Jo drew a family tree for all the relatives of Harry's godfather, Sirius Black. The picture was bought by the mother of Daniel Radcliffe, who played Harry Potter in the movies.

The best part was knowing that children all over the world were reading her stories and loving them. Years after the last book was published, Jo was still getting hundreds of letters every day from people who loved Harry. She answered every one with the help of two secretaries.

In 2011, her fans got another surprise when Jo announced a new website, Pottermore.

Pottermore was "an online reading experience unlike any other," where readers could participate in Harry's story themselves. People who signed into the site could take a quiz written by Jo herself that sorted them into one of the four houses of Hogwarts. They could choose a magical pet and

THE INTERNET

IN THE LATE 1990S, THE BUDDING INTERNET GAVE HARRY POTTER FANS A WAY OF CONNECTING AND TALKING TO ONE ANOTHER FROM ALL CORNERS OF THE WORLD. NOW FANS HAD CHAT ROOMS AND MESSAGE BOARDS. FANS CREATED WEBSITES ABOUT THEIR FAVORITE CHARACTERS. JO HERSELF SOMETIMES CHECKED THE FAN-CREATED HARRY POTTER LEXICON SITE, WHICH CATALOGUED EVERYTHING IN THE BOOKS FOR EASY REFERENCE. OTHER SITES LIKE FICTIONALLEY, MUGGLENET, AND THE LEAKY CAULDRON GAVE FANS A PLACE TO SHARE THEIR OWN ARTWORK AND STORIES ABOUT THE HARRY POTTER CHARACTERS. USING THE INTERNET, FANS WERE ALSO ABLE TO PLAN CONVENTIONS LIKE NIMBUS, PHOENIX RISING, AND SECTUS, WHERE THEY MET IN DIFFERENT CITIES TO TALK ABOUT HARRY POTTER.

be chosen by a magic wand. The site was also full of extra information that Jo couldn't find a place for in the books themselves. For instance, she filled in information on characters' early lives before they made their appearances in the books. The site also had artwork showing scenes from the books—down to the last detail. Jo supervised everything so that it would look exactly how she imagined. Every person who entered the site entered Harry's world. Perhaps one day some of her fans would become authors and write their own stories. For Jo Rowling, that would be truly magical.

However much her life had changed, Jo was still a writer. Each day her husband went to work as a doctor. Jo fed David and Mackenzie and went to her small office in her house in Edinburgh to write. At lunchtime she made herself a sandwich. Then she returned to writing until Jessica came home from school.

But what was Jo writing? That's what everyone wanted to know, and she wasn't telling. "I think I always felt I didn't want to publish again until the last film was out because Potter has been such a huge thing in my life," she told BBC News. "I've been writing hard ever since I finished writing *Hallows*, so I've got a lot of stuff and I suppose it's a question of deciding which one comes out first. But I will publish again. In a sense it's a beginning for me as well as an end."

Then, in February 2012, word was out. Little, Brown Book Group, a publishing company in the United Kingdom, announced a new book by J. K. Rowling. It was for grown-ups, not children. Jo said the new book will be "very different to the Harry Potter series, although I've enjoyed writing it every bit as much." She didn't give any details about the story, but Jo had already decided that it would not be about magic. "I think I've done my fantasy," Jo said. "To go and create another fantasy universe would feel wrong, and I don't know if I'm capable of it."

Jo might have finished writing Harry Potter, but chances are that kids will continue to read about him for generations to come. Harry's world of dragons, castles, and magic wands is truly timeless. Perhaps one day he will take his place among other classic children's book characters like Peter Pan and Alice in Wonderland, with his story read by children of all ages forever.

TIMELINE OF
J. K. ROWLING'S LIFE

1965 —— Joanne is born in Gloucestershire, England

1971 —— Writes a story about her sister, Di, falling down a rabbit hole

1974 —— Family moves to Tutshill

1980 —— Mother is diagnosed with multiple sclerosis

1983 —— Goes to the University of Exeter

1990 —— Harry Potter pops into her head during a train trip
Mother dies

1992 —— Marries Jorge Arantes in Portugal

1993 —— Daughter Jessica is born
Gets a divorce and moves back to Edinburgh

1997 —— *Harry Potter and the Philosopher's Stone* is published in the UK

1998 —— *Harry Potter and the Sorcerer's Stone* is published in the US

2001 —— Writes two charity books, *Quidditch Through the Ages* and *Fantastic Beasts and Where to Find Them* in March
First Harry Potter movie premieres in November
Marries Neil Murray in December

2003 —— Son, David, is born

2005 —— Daughter Mackenzie is born

2007 —— *Harry Potter and the Deathly Hallows*, the final Harry Potter book, is published in July

TIMELINE OF
THE WORLD

Town of Salem, Massachusetts, holds a series of witch trials — **1692**

Jane Austen publishes *Emma* — **1815**

Alice in Wonderland by Lewis Carroll is published — **1865**

The Fellowship of the Ring, the first volume of *The Lord of the Rings* by J. R. R. Tolkien, is published — **1954**

The TV remote control is invented — **1956**

Dr. Martin Luther King, Jr., delivers his "I Have a Dream" speech in Washington, DC — **1963**

Beatlemania hits America
TV series *Bewitched* premieres — **1964**

First moon landing occurs — **1969**

Fall of Saigon ends the Vietnam War — **1975**

Star Wars opens — **1977**

Prince Charles marries Lady Diana Spencer — **1981**

Berlin Wall falls — **1989**

Chunnel, an underground tunnel connecting England and France, is opened — **1994**

Terrorist attack destroys the World Trade Center in New York City
The iPod is unveiled — **2001**

Twilight is published — **2005**

Pluto is reclassified as a dwarf planet — **2006**

BIBLIOGRAPHY

"The Harry Potter Economy," *The Economist*, December 19, 2009, http://www.economist.com/node/15108711.

"JK Rowling, Learning To Live With Fame, Fortune and Life Without Harry," *The Independent*, July 8, 2007, http://www.independent.co.uk/arts-entertainment/books/features/jk-rowling-learning-to-live-with-fame-fortune-and-life-without-harry-456091.html.

DanRadcliffe.com. "Biography." http://www.danradcliffe.com/index.php?option=com_content&view=article&id=15&Itemid=16. Accessed August 1, 2011.

Emma Watson Official Site. "Life & Emma." http://www.emmawatson.com/en/Emma/About/. Accessed August 1, 2011.

J. K. Rowling Official Site. "Biography." http://www.jkrowling.com/textonly/en/biography.cfm. Accessed August 1, 2011.

Nel, Phil. **J K Rowling's Harry Potter Novels**. New York: Continuum International Publishing Group, 2001.

Rowling, J. K. "The Not Especially Fascinating Life So Far of J. K. Rowling." http://www.accio-quote.org/articles/1998/autobiography.html. Accessed August 1, 2011.

Vos MacDonald, Joan. **J. K. Rowling: Banned, Challenged, and Censored**. Berkeley Heights, NJ: Enslow Publishers, 2008.

The Worldwide Home for Rupert Grint Fans. "Rupert Grint: Biography." http://www.rupertgrint.net/rupert-grint-biography. Accessed August 1, 2011.

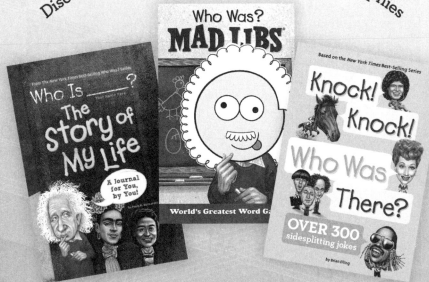